In memory of my mother, Mary French,
and for Henry and Priscilla McDougall,
Tim and Ann Riviere,
and Richard and Inge Spurrell

Bethlehem
Copyright © 2001 Frances Lincoln Limited
Text and illustrations copyright © 2001 Fiona French
Printed in Singapore. All rights reserved.
www.harperchildrens.com

Library of Congress Cataloging-in-Publication Data is available.
ISBN 0-06-029623-2

1 2 3 4 5 6 7 8 9 10
❖
First HarperCollins Edition, 2001
First published in the United Kingdom by Frances Lincoln Limited, 2001

Fiona French

Bethlehem

With Words from the Authorized Version of the
King James Bible

HarperCollins*Publishers*

And it came to pass in those days, that there went out a decree from Caesar Augustus, that all the world should be taxed. And all went to be taxed, every one into his own city.

And Joseph also went up from Galilee, out of the city of Nazareth, into Judaea, unto the city of David, which is called Bethlehem, to be taxed with Mary his espoused wife, being great with child.

And so it was, that, while they were there, the days were accomplished that she should be delivered. And she brought forth her firstborn son, and wrapped him in swaddling clothes, and laid him in a manger, because there was no room for them in the inn.

And there were in the same country
shepherds abiding in the field,
keeping watch over their flock by night.

And, lo, the angel of the Lord came upon them, and the glory of the Lord shone about them: and they were sore afraid.

And the angel said unto them, "Fear not: for, behold, I bring you good tidings of great joy, which shall be to all people. For unto you is born this day in the city of David a Saviour, which is Christ the Lord."

And there were in the same country
shepherds abiding in the field,
keeping watch over their flock by night.

And, lo, the angel of the Lord came upon them, and the glory of the Lord shone about them: and they were sore afraid.

And the angel said unto them, "Fear not: for, behold, I bring you good tidings of great joy, which shall be to all people. For unto you is born this day in the city of David a Saviour, which is Christ the Lord."

And suddenly there was with the angel a multitude of the heavenly host praising God, and saying, "Glory to God in the highest, and on earth peace, good will toward men."

The shepherds said one to another, "Let us now go even unto Bethlehem, and see this thing which is come to pass." And they came with haste, and found Mary, and Joseph, and the babe lying in a manger.

Now when Jesus was born in Bethlehem of Judaea in the days of Herod the king, behold, there came wise men from the east to Jerusalem, saying, "Where is he that is born King of the Jews? for we have seen his star in the east, and are come to worship him."

And, lo, the star, which they saw in the east, went before them, till it came and stood over where the young child was. And when they saw the young child with Mary his mother, they fell down and worshipped him: and presented unto him gifts: gold, and frankincense, and myrrh.

And being warned of God in
a dream that they should not
return to Herod, they departed into
their own country another way.

And behold, the angel of the Lord appeared to Joseph in a dream, saying, "Arise, and take the young child and his mother, and flee into Egypt, and be thou there until I bring thee word: for Herod will seek the young child to destroy him."

When Joseph arose, he took the
young child and his mother
by night, and departed into Egypt:
And was there until the death of Herod:
that it might be fulfilled which was spoken
of the Lord by the prophet, saying,
"Out of Egypt have I called my son."